INTRODUCTION

We have worked with thousands of families and individuals just like you, and with the advantage of years of experience and legal knowledge, have created this book to help you and your family.

This Private Information Guide is intended to serve as one place to record your most important personal, legal, financial, and medical information, so it is at the fingertips of those you entrust to handle your medical and financial matters in case anything happens to you. Even if you have your estate planning documents in place, your trusted agent's, personal representative's or trustee's job is made so much harder if information has not been organized.

Do not leave your family lost with no direction or information. This gift of information and organization will help to ensure continuity of your medical care and management of your financial matters in case you suffer a serious illness or injury, and allow for much easier and efficient administration of your affairs at end of life. We have designed this book to help you leave a legacy, and not a mess.

To organize your information and records:

- Complete this book;
- Keep the book in a secure location with your estate planning, legal, and other important documents;
- Let at least one person know where to find this book; and
- Update information as needed.

ISBN: 978-1-7338436-0-7 (Paperback Edition)

Printed and bound in the United States of America

TABLE OF CONTENTS

PERSONAL INFORMATION

In case of an emergency or death, your family, friends and professional advisors will need vital, timely information. Please complete this section to provide details regarding your family, emergency contacts, employment, and location of important documents.

PERSONAL INFORMATION

	Self	Spouse	Mother	Father
First Name				
Middle Name				
Last Name				
Maiden Name				
Marital Status				
Date of Birth				
Birthplace City, State, County				
Email				
Address City, State, County				
Cell Number				
Work Number				
Home Number				
Social Security #				
Driver' License # and State				
US Military Service/ Branch				

ADDITIONAL NOTES

INFORMATION - CHILDREN

	Child #1	Child #2	Child #3	Child #4	Child #5
First Name					
Middle Name					
Last Name					
Maiden Name					
Date of Birth					
Birthplace City, State, County					
Email					
Address City, State, County					
Cellular Number					
Work Number					
Home Number					
Social Security #					
Driver' License # and State					
US Military Service/ Branch					
Married?	☐ Yes ☐ No	☐ Yes ☐ No	☐ Yes ☐ No	☐ Yes ☐ No	☐ Yes ☐ No
Name of Spouse					

ADDITIONAL NOTES

INFORMATION - SIBLINGS

	Sibling #1	Sbling #2	Sibling #3	Sibling #4	Sibling #5
First Name					
Middle Name					
Last Name					
Maiden Name					
Date of Birth					
Birthplace City, State, County					
Email					
Address City, State, County					
Cellular Number					
Work Number					
Home Number					
Social Security #					
Driver' License # and State					
US Military Service/ Branch					
Married?	☐ Yes ☐ No	☐ Yes ☐ No	☐ Yes ☐ No	☐ Yes ☐ No	☐ Yes ☐ No
Name of Spouse					

ADDITIONAL NOTES

INFORMATION - GRANDCHILDREN

	Grandchild #1	Grandchild #2	Grandchild #3	Grandchild #4
Parents Name				
Child's Legal Name				
Current Residence City and State				
Maiden Name				
Date of Birth				
Birthplace City, State, County				
Email				
Address City, State, County				
Cellular Number				
Work Number				
Home Number				
Social Security #				
Driver' License # and State				
US Military Service/ Branch				

ADDITIONAL NOTES

INFORMATION - OTHER

	Other	**Other**	**Other**	**Other**	**Other**
First Name					
Middle Name					
Last Name					
Maiden Name					
Date of Birth					
Birthplace City, State, County					
Email					
Address City, State, County					
Cellular Number					
Work Number					
Home Number					
Social Security #					
Driver' License # and State					
US Military Service/ Branch					

ADDITIONAL NOTES

EMERGENCY CONTACTS

Name	Relationship	Phone Number and Email Address	Mailing Address

ADDITIONAL NOTES

EMERGENCY CONTACTS (Cont'd)

Name	**Relationship**	**Phone Number and Email Address**	**Mailing Address**

ADDITIONAL NOTES

PROFESSIONAL CONTACTS

Name	**Profession**	**Phone Number and Email Address**	**Mailing Address**
Attorney			
Attorney			
Financial Advisor			
Tax Preparer			
Insurance Agent			
Clergy			

ADDITIONAL NOTES

PROFESSIONAL CONTACTS (Cont'd)

Name	Profession	Phone Number and Email Address	Mailing Address

ADDITIONAL NOTES

EMPLOYMENT INFORMATION

Name of Employer	Phone Number	Mailing Address	Position	Benefits
Start Date	End Date		Ownership Interest	Yes (_____) % No _____
Name of Employer	Phone Number	Mailing Address	Position	Benefits
Start Date	End Date		Ownership Interest	Yes (_____) % No _____
Name of Employer	Phone Number	Mailing Address	Position	Benefits
Start Date	End Date		Ownership Interest	Yes (_____) % No _____
Name of Employer	Phone Number	Mailing Address	Position	Benefits
Start Date	End Date		Ownership Interest	Yes (_____) % No _____
Name of Employer	Phone Number	Mailing Address	Position	Benefits
Start Date	End Date		Ownership Interest	Yes (_____) % No _____

EMPLOYMENT INFORMATION (Cont'd)

Name of Employer	Phone Number	Mailing Address	Position	Benefits
Start Date	End Date		Ownership Interest	Yes (_____) % No _____
Name of Employer	Phone Number	Mailing Address	Position	Benefits
Start Date	End Date		Ownership Interest	Yes (_____) % No _____
Name of Employer	Phone Number	Mailing Address	Position	Benefits
Start Date	End Date		Ownership Interest	Yes (_____) % No _____

ADDITIONAL NOTES

IMPORTANT DOCUMENTS

Documents	Where is this document stored?	Person Who Has a Copy	Notes
Birth Certificate			
Social Security Card			
Marriage Certificates			
Divorce Decrees			
Naturalization Certificates			
Citizenship Papers			
Military Discharge			
Veteran Papers			
Diploma/Transcripts			
Life Insurance Policies			
Retirement Plan			
Stock Certificates			
Bonds			
Real Estate Deeds			
Annuity Contracts			
Immunization Records			
Living Will			
Last Will and Testament			
Healthcare Power of Attorney			
Financial Power of Attorney			
Trust(s)			

IMPORTANT DOCUMENTS (Cont'd)

Documents	Where is this document stored?	Person Who Has a Copy	Notes
Lawsuit Documents			
Employment Contracts			
Burial Instructions			
Cemetery Deed			
Prenuptial Agreement			
Safe Deposit Box Inventory			
Household Inventory			
Photos of Possessions			

MEDICAL INFORMATION

Your caregivers and medical decision makers will need your health insurance and medical provider information, as well as basic medical history, to be your best advocate. Please complete this section to make sure things do not get missed. For individuals with significant medical history or conditions, you may also wish to keep a separate notebook with copies of medical results, records, and medication list, or use a website, or app to store personal health records online.

HEALTH INSURANCE

Insurer	Plan ID	Group #	Medicare #
Medigap/Supplemental Plan Name			
Prescription Coverage	Issuer	Group #	ID #
Prescription Coverage (Medicare D)	Issuer	Group #	ID #
Blood Type	☐ O ☐ A	☐ B ☐ AB	☐ Positive ☐ Negative
VA Medical	☐ Yes ☐ No	Group #	ID #

ADDITIONAL NOTES

MEDICAL HISTORY and ALLERGIES

MEDICAL HISTORY – Please check all that apply:

☐ No known medical conditions	☐ Diabetes/Insulin Dependent	☐ Seizure Disorder
☐ Abnormal EKG	☐ Eye Surgery	☐ Sickle Cell Anemia
☐ Alzheimer's	☐ Glaucoma	☐ Stroke/CYA/TIA
☐ Angina	☐ Hearing Impaired	☐ UTI
☐ Asthma/Emphysema	☐ Heart Valve Prosthesis	☐ Vision Impaired
☐ Bleeding Disorder	☐ Hemodialysis	☐
☐ CABG	☐ Hemolytic Anemia	☐
☐ Cancer	☐ Hypertension	☐
☐ Cardiac Dysrhythmia	☐ Leukemia	☐
☐ Cataracts	☐ LVAD	☐
☐ CHF	☐ Myasthenia Gravis	☐
☐ Clotting Disorder	☐ Myocardial Infarct	☐
☐ COPD	☐ Pacemaker/Defib	☐
☐ Coronary Bypass Stent	☐ Pneumonia	☐
☐ Dementia	☐ Renal Failure	☐

ALLERGIES – Please check all that apply:

☐ No known allergies	☐ Insect Stings	☐
☐ Aspirin	☐ Latex	☐
☐ Barbiturates	☐ Lidocaine	☐
☐ Codeine	☐ Morphine	☐
☐ Demerol	☐ Novocaine	☐
☐ Environmental	☐ Penicillin	☐
☐ Horse Serum	☐ X-Rays/Dyes	☐

RECENT SURGERIES

Dates	Procedures

MEDICATIONS

Medications	Dosage	Frequency	Reason for medication	Who prescribed medication

ADDITIONAL NOTES

MEDICAL SERVICE PROVIDERS

Name of Physician and Specialty	Contact Information (Phone number and address)
Name of Physician and Specialty	Contact Information (Phone number and address)
Name of Physician and Specialty	Contact Information (Phone number and address)
Name of Physician and Specialty	Contact Information (Phone number and address)
Name of Physician and Specialty	Contact Information (Phone number and address)

ADDITIONAL NOTES

MEDICAL SERVICE PROVIDERS (Cont'd)

Home Health	Contact Information (Phone number and address)
Hospice	Contact Information (Phone number and address)
Physical Therapy	Contact Information (Phone number and address)
Speech Therapy	Contact Information (Phone number and address)
Occupational Therapy	Contact Information (Phone number and address)

ADDITIONAL NOTES

FINANCIAL MATTERS

Keeping financial information organized and readily available is one of the most helpful gifts you can give to those you care about. Please complete the information in this section as it applies to you, and update regularly.

BANK ACCOUNTS

BANK ACCOUNTS – e.g., Checking, Savings, C.D., and Money Market

Name of Bank	**Type of Account**	**Name on Account**	**Account Number**	**Pin #**

CREDIT CARD ACCOUNTS

Type of Card/ Issuer	Name on Account	Account #	Monthly Due Date

ADDITIONAL NOTES

INVESTMENT ACCOUNTS

NON-RETIREMENT INVESTMENT ACCOUNTS - e.g., Brokerage, currency or other accounts

Account #	Financial Advisor	Phone #
Institution	Account Type	Name on Account
Account #	Financial Advisor	Phone #
Institution	Account Type	Name on Account
Account #	Financial Advisor	Phone #
Institution	Account Type	Name on Account
Account #	Financial Advisor	Phone #
Institution	Account Type	Name on Account
Account #	Financial Advisor	Phone #
Institution	Account Type	Name on Account

STOCKS and BONDS

STOCK CERTIFICATES

Name of Company	Contact Information	Name on Certificate	Number of Shares
Location of Stock Certificates:			

BONDS

Type of Bond	Series	Name on Bonds	Face Value
Location of Bonds:			

RETIREMENT ACCOUNTS

RETIREMENT ACCOUNTS – e.g., IRA, 401K, SEP IRA, etc.

Type of Account	**Account Number**	**Institution Name, Advisor Name and Phone Number**	**Beneficiary Designations**

INSURANCE POLICIES

LIFE INSURANCE POLICIES

Type of Policy	Company Name and Phone Number	Name on Account (Insured/Policy Owner)	Death Benefit - Cash Value	Beneficiary Designation
Policy #		Agent	Agent Phone #	
Type of Policy	Company Name and Phone Number	Name on Account (Insured/Policy Owner)	Death Benefit - Cash Value	Beneficiary Designation
Policy #		Agent	Agent Phone #	
Type of Policy	Company Name and Phone Number	Name on Account (Insured/Policy Owner)	Death Benefit - Cash Value	Beneficiary Designation
Policy #		Agent	Agent Phone #	

LONG TERM CARE POLICY

Type of Policy	Company Name and Phone Number	Name on Account (Insured/Policy Owner)	Information
Policy #		Agent	Agent Phone #

BUSINESS INTERESTS

Name of Business	Contact Numbers	Mailing Address	Position	
Type of Business		Job Title or Position	Ownership Interest	
Name of Business	Contact Numbers	Mailing Address	Position	
Type of Business		Job Title or Position	Ownership Interest	
Name of Business	Contact Numbers	Mailing Address	Position	
Type of Business		Job Title or Position	Ownership Interest	
Name of Employer	Contact Numbers	Mailing Address	Position	
Type of Business		Job Title or Position	Ownership Interest	

ADDITIONAL NOTES

BUSINESS INTERESTS (Cont'd)

Name of Business	Contact Numbers	Mailing Address	Position	
Type of Business		Job Title or Position	Ownership Interest	
Name of Business	Contact Numbers	Mailing Address	Position	
Type of Business		Job Title or Position	Ownership Interest	
Name of Business	Contact Numbers	Mailing Address	Position	
Type of Business		Job Title or Position	Ownership Interest	
Name of Employer	Contact Numbers	Mailing Address	Position	
Type of Business		Job Title or Position	Ownership Interest	

ADDITIONAL NOTES

SAFE DEPOSIT BOXES

SAFE DEPOSIT BOXES

Location	Box #	Name on Account	Key or Combination	Additional Comments/ Location of Key
			☐ Key ☐ Combination	
			☐ Key ☐ Combination	
			☐ Key ☐ Combination	
			☐ Key ☐ Combination	
			☐ Key ☐ Combination	
			Other	
			Other	
			Other	

ADDITIONAL NOTES

REAL PROPERTY

Primary Residence ☐ Own ☐ Rent	Physical Address, City, State and Zip
If Own, Name(s) on the Title	
If Rent, Name of Management Co.	
Secondary Property ☐ Own ☐ Rent	Physical Address, City, State and Zip
If Own, Name(s) on the Title	
If Rent, Name of Management Co.	
Other Property ☐ Own ☐ Rent	Physical Address, City, State and Zip
If Own, Name(s) on the Title	
If Rent, Name of Management Co.	
Other Property ☐ Own ☐ Rent	Physical Address, City, State and Zip
If Own, Name(s) on the Title	
If Rent, Name of Management Co.	

REAL PROPERTY (Cont'd)

Property	Insurance Company	PolicyNumber	Agent's Name and Number
Primary Property			
HOA ☐ Yes ☐ No	HOA Contact Info.		
Secondary Property			
HOA ☐ Yes ☐ No	HOA Contact Info.		
Other Property			
HOA ☐ Yes ☐ No	HOA Contact Info.		
Other Property			
HOA ☐ Yes ☐ No	HOA Contact Info.		

ADDITIONAL NOTES

PROPERTY INFORMATION

Company Name	Utility/Vendor	Contact Numbers	Account Number

ADDITIONAL NOTES

PROPERTY INFORMATION

Utility Company	Account Name	Account Number	Contact Information
Gas Company	Account Name	Account Number	Contact Information
Water Company	Account Name	Account Number	Contact Information
Trash/Recycle Co.	Account Name	Account Number	Contact Information
Cable Company	Account Name	Account Number	Contact Information
Landline Company	Account Name	Account Number	Contact Information
Cellular Company	Account Name	Account Number	Contact Information
Landscape Company	Account Name	Account Number	Contact Information
Pool Company	Account Name	Account Number	Contact Information
Electrician	Account Name	Account Number	Contact Information
Plumber	Account Name	Account Number	Contact Information
Other	Account Name	Account Number	Contact Information
Other	Account Name	Account Number	Contact Information
Other	Account Name	Account Number	Contact Information
Other	Account Name	Account Number	Contact Information

OTHER INFORMATION

Newspaper	Account Name	Account Number	Contact Information
Babysitter #1	Account Name	Account Number	Contact Information
Babysitter #2	Account Name	Account Number	Contact Information
Electrician	Account Name	Account Number	Contact Information
Plumber	Account Name	Account Number	Contact Information
Other	Account Name	Account Number	Contact Information
Other	Account Name	Account Number	Contact Information
Other	Account Name	Account Number	Contact Information
Other	Account Name	Account Number	Contact Information
Other	Account Name	Account Number	Contact Information
Other	Account Name	Account Number	Contact Information
Other	Account Name	Account Number	Contact Information

VEHICLE INFORMATION

CARS, BOATS, TRUCKS, TRAILERS, etc.

Year	Make/Model	License Plate	Vin #	Name on Title	Financed
					☐ Yes ☐ No
					☐ Yes ☐ No
					☐ Yes ☐ No
					☐ Yes ☐ No
					☐ Yes ☐ No
					☐ Yes ☐ No

VEHICLE LOANS

Vehicle	Lender Name	Loan #	Lender Contact Info	Due Date

VEHICLE INSURANCE

Vehicle	Ins. Company	Policy #	Contact Info.	Due Date

FINANCIAL PASSWORDS

ONLINE PASSWORDS

Type of Account	Account Name and Phone Number	User ID/Password Access Online Info	Pin #
Credit Card			
Credit Card			
Credit Card			
Credit Card			
Checking			
Checking			
Savings			
Mortgage			
Mortgage			
Home Equity Loan			
Other			
Other			

SECURED SERVICES and PASSWORDS

Service or Program	Account Name/URL	User ID/Password	Pin#
Amazon			
Facebook			
Hulu			
Instagram			
Linked In			
Netflix			
Cable			
Internet			
Computer			
Cellular Phone			

ADDITIONAL NOTES

SECURED SERVICES and PASSWORDS

Service or Program	Account Name/URL	User ID/Password Access Online Info	Pin #

WARRANTY INFORMATION

Item Covered Under Warranty	Warranty Number	Where Original Documents Found	When Expires

MEMBERSHIPS and COMMUNITIES

Name of Organization	Contact Name	Account or Membership Number	ID and Password	Position
Name of Organization	Contact Name	Account or Membership Number	ID and Password	Position
Name of Organization	Contact Name	Account or Membership Number	ID and Password	Position
Name of Organization	Contact Name	Account or Membership Number	ID and Password	Position
Name of Organization	Contact Name	Account or Membership Number	ID and Password	Position
Name of Organization	Contact Name	Account or Membership Number	ID and Password	Position

ADDITIONAL NOTES

LEGAL DOCUMENTS

Estate planning documents designate individuals or entities to handle medical and financial matters during lifetime, as may be needed, and to administer your estate/trust. Please complete this section with the contact information for those you have designated. It is important you have the right estate planning documents in place, and update them regularly with an experienced estate planning attorney. In addition, you need to be certain the ownership and beneficiary designations on your accounts and assets are consistent with your estate planning wishes. Proper estate planning is much more than just a Will. Please seek advice of counsel. Without proper planning, there may be unnecessary legal proceedings, delays, expenses, family conflict, or undesired outcomes.

ESTATE PLANNING DOCUMENTS

MEDICAL DIRECTIVES and POWERS OF ATTORNEY

Health Care Power of Attorney, Living Will, HIPAA Release, Do Not Resuscitate, etc.

Document Title	
Date Executed	
First Agent(s) Name/Contact Info	
Alternate Agent(s) Name/Contact Info	
Document Title	
Date Executed	
First Agent(s) Name/Contact Info	
Alternate Agents' Name/Contact Info	
Document Title	
Date Executed	
First Agent(s) Name/Contact Info	
Alternate Agent(s) Name/Contact Info	
Document Title	
Date Executed	
First Agent(s) Name/Contact Info	
Alternate Agent(s) Name/Contact Info	

ESTATE PLANNING (Cont'd)

MEDICAL DIRECTIVES and POWERS OF ATTORNEY

Health Care Power of Attorney, Living Will, HIPAA Release, Do Not Resuscitate, etc.

Document Title	
Date Executed	
First Agent(s) Name/Contact Info	
Alternate Agent(s) Name/Contact Info	

FINANCIAL POWERS OF ATTORNEY

Document Title	
Date Executed	
First Agent(s) Name/Contact Info	
Alternate Agent(s) Name/Contact Info	

ADDITIONAL NOTES

ESTATE PLANNING (Cont'd)

LAST WILL and TESTAMENT

Last Will and Testament	
Date Executed	
Dates of all Codicils to Will	
First Personal Representative Name/Contact Info	
Alternate 1 Name/Contact Info	
Alternate 2 Name/Contact Info	
Alternate 3 Name/Contact Info	

TRUSTS

Name of Trust	
Date Executed	
Dates of all Amendments	
First Name/Contact Info	
Alternate 1 Name/Contact Info	
Alternate 2 Name/Contact Info	
Alternate 3 Name/Contact Info	

GOVERNMENT BENEFITS and MILITARY SERVICE

Original copies of military records and government benefits information should be safeguarded. In particular, the DD-214 or other military discharge paperwork may be required for VA healthcare eligibility, education benefits with the GI Bill, VA loans, Aid and Attendance Pension benefits, and military burial.

GOVERNMENT BENEFITS

INCOME

Social Security	Monthly Benefit Amt.	Deposited Into Acct.
☐ Retirement ☐ Disability (SSDI) ☐ Supplemental Security Income (SSI) ☐ Dependent Adult Child (DAC)		
Representative (if any) Payee Name and Contact Information		

VETERANS BENEFITS

Veterans Benefits	Monthly Benefit Amt.	Deposited Into Acct.
☐ Pension ☐ Disability ☐ Aid and Attendance Pension Benefits		
VA Fiduciary (if any) Name and Contact Information		

STATE or FEDERAL GOVERNMENT PENSION

State or Federal	Monthly Benefit Amt.	Deposited Into Acct.
Payee Name and Contact Information		

OTHER

☐ Medicare	☐ Medicaid Health Ins.	☐ Medicaid Long Term Care	
☐ HUD	☐ SNAP		

MILITARY SERVICE

Full Name Enlisted	
Which Military Branch	
Date Enlisted	
Date Discharged	
Final Rank	
Service Military Disability Rating, (if any)	

Do you have your DD-214 Form (Service Record)?	☐ Yes	☐ No
Where are your Military Discharge documents located?		

ADDITIONAL NOTES

PETS

If you have pets, you probably consider them family and want to be sure they would be well taken care of if you could no longer do so yourself. Complete this section to provide information about your pets and desired caretakers. Note, most states allow pet trusts to be established to pay for the care of your pets; seek advice of legal counsel for more information.

INFORMATION - PETS

Name	Breed/Species	Has a Chip? ☐ Yes ☐ No Chip ID #	Coloring
Who should care for your pet in the event of your death? Name Phone #			
Veterinary's Name and Address		Phone #	
Name	Breed/Species	Has a Chip? ☐ Yes ☐ No Chip ID #	Coloring
Who should care for your pet in the event of your death? Name Phone #			
Veterinary's Name and Address		Phone #	
Name	Breed/Species	Has a Chip? ☐ Yes ☐ No Chip ID #	Coloring
Who should care for your pet in the event of your death? Name Phone #			
Veterinary's Name and Address		Phone #	

ADDITIONAL NOTES

INFORMATION - PETS (Cont'd)

Name	Breed/Species	Has a Chip? ☐ Yes ☐ No Chip ID #	Coloring
Who should care for your pet in the event of your death? Name Phone #			
Veterinary's Name and Address		Phone #	
Name	Breed/Species	Has a Chip? ☐ Yes ☐ No Chip ID #	Coloring
Who should care for your pet in the event of your death? Name Phone #			
Veterinary's Name and Address		Phone #	
Name	Breed/Species	Has a Chip? ☐ Yes ☐ No Chip ID #	Coloring
Who should care for your pet in the event of your death? Name Phone #			
Veterinary's Name and Address		Phone #	

ADDITIONAL NOTES

FINAL WISHES

During a period of your incapacity or in the event of your death, your loved ones are often not able to think clearly. Some decisions must be made within hours of death. Any guidance you can provide will help and reduce potential conflict.

You may want to include your burial or cremation wishes and a description of the kind of memorial service you would like, if any. You may also want to express your feelings about the general amounts that should be spent for these remembrances. Or, you may have made pre-arrangements that should be described.

FINAL WISHES INFORMATION

Pre-Paid Burial Contract ☐ Yes ☐ No	If yes, name of company, contact information and policy number
	If no, it is my desire for:

☐ **Burial**			
	Check One: ☐ Immediate ☐ After services	Check One: ☐ Embalm ☐ Do not embalm	Check One: ☐ In-ground ☐ Above-ground
Funeral Home Mortuary Cemetery	Name	Address	Phone #
Burial Plot Location		**Description**	**Plot #**
☐ **Cremation**			
	Check One: ☐ Embalm ☐ Do not embalm	Check One: ☐ Niche in Columbarium ☐ In-ground	Check One: ☐ Scattered ☐ To individual
Funeral Home Mortuary Cemetery	Name	Address	Phone #

MEMORIAL SERVICE and ADDITIONAL NOTES and INSTRUCTIONS

SERVICE INFORMATION

Religious memberships and beliefs are as follows;
I desire that services be: ☐ for friends and relatives, or ☐ private
Description of any pre-purchased plans or description of wishes;
Clergy
Pallbearers
Scripture selections
Music selections
Other

STEPHANIE A. BIVENS, Esq., C.E.L.A.
Author

Certified Elder Law Attorney by the National Elder Law Foundation (NELF), accredited by the State Bar of Arizona.

An Arizona native, Ms. Bivens has over 20 years legal experience in estate planning, probate and trust administration, elder law, and special needs planning. As an award winning, nationally and locally recognized attorney in her field, Ms. Bivens maintains an active law practice as managing attorney of Bivens & Associates, P.L.L.C., and is a frequent speaker and writer. She devotes her time, knowledge, and passion to working with individuals, families, licensed fiduciaries, banks and trust companies.

Ms. Bivens is married with two adult children, has two dogs and a cat. She enjoys horseback riding, hiking, and traveling, and resides in Scottsdale, Arizona.

DISCLAIMER: *The author and publisher are providing this book and its contents on an "as is" basis and make no representations or warranties of any kind with respect to this book or its contents. The author and publisher disclaim all such representations and warranties, including for example warranties of educational, medical, legal, or financial advice. The author and publisher do not represent or warrant that the information added to this book is accurate, complete or current. The owner of this book is solely responsible for the confidential information contained in this book, and the security of said book and its contents. Neither the author or publisher, nor any authors, contributors, or other representatives, will be liable for damages arising out of or in connection with the use of this book.*

Use of this book implies your acceptance of this disclaimer. This book is not intended as a substitute for consultation with licensed medical, legal, or financial professionals. Possession or use of this book shall not constitute the establishment of an attorney/client relationship or legal advice. The personalized information that is added to the Private Information Guide by its owner has not been evaluated, approved, or otherwise recommended or reviewed by author and publisher.

Made in the USA
Monee, IL
05 November 2026

67386572R00043